Y'ALL HIRING?

Y'ALL HIRING?

The Black Teen's Guide to Navigating Employment

Albert Phillips Jr.

Library of Congress Control Number: 2020916304
Paperback ISBN: 978-1-7353247-0-8
Ebook ISBN: 978-1-7353247-1-5

Cover design by Mikea Hugley
Interior design by Liz Schrieter
Editing and production by Reading List Editorial:
readinglisteditorial.com

For media inquiries, booking, or information about special
discounts for bulk purchases, please email
hello@albertphillipsjr.com.

This book is dedicated to Black youth of the world. You are valuable. You are omnipotent. You are a blessing. You are exactly what our ancestors prayed and sacrificed for.

This book is also dedicated to Edward Graves Jr. The world lost you far too soon, and I think about you every day. I want you to take it back to '04 in heaven and throw on a 3X white tee for old times' sake. I miss you, man.

Contents

Part 3: Exit Your Job Like a Boss   65

Preface:
The Story Behind
This Book

During one of those blistering-hot summer days of 2006, I was bored sitting in my house, thinking, "Man, I need some paper!" I was a teenager living in Cedonia, a neighborhood in northeast Baltimore, and I was tired of asking my dad for money. I wanted to buy my own PlayStation video games and fresh gear from Eastpoint Mall. I also dreamed of saving to get my own car and using it to flex at school next fall and to travel more easily through the city. I wanted it on my own—by my own terms. To remedy my financial burden, I decided to walk up to the Foot Locker in Erdman Shopping Center and apply for a Sales Associate position. I thought, "How hard could it be to get a position at my favorite shoe retailer?" I'd had other part-time jobs in the past, so I figured this would be a breeze.

When I walked in the door, the staff just paused and looked at me for a moment. It was like I just got dropped off by a spaceship. I am sure the confused looks were the result of my appearance. I had cornrows at the time, and one half of my hair was styled like a young Meek Mill's, with braids that locked, and the other half was out in an afro like Huey from *The Boondocks*. My bottom half consisted of ripped jean shorts and some Air Force 1's. My top half sported a throwback basketball jersey. Needless to say, my appearance seemed out of place for a job seeker.

Upon entering, I said the words that employers are completely tired of hearing from applicants: "Y'all hiring?" The lady behind the register screwed up her face, clearly disgusted, and said, "Yes, we are, but we don't have any applications." I guess she thought that would cause me to become disinterested. Instead, I told her I would be back later with a completed one.

After I left, I grabbed a chicken box from a spot a few stores up and then headed back home. After I smashed my food, I worked to avoid a food coma by finding a digital copy of Foot Locker's application online. Next, I printed it out, completed it, and trekked back to the shoe store to drop it off.

The manager, the same woman who gave me the crazy look earlier, accepted my application, but I never received a call, and I never followed up about the status of my application. I assume she balled it up and took a long-range shot into a faraway trashcan. She probably even mimicked the moves of the player whose jersey I was wearing when attempting the basket and yelled out "Kobe" before sinking the shot.

This was my first memorable experience of job hunting. I was never schooled on how to navigate the employment terrain, so I did what I thought was best. I mean, I printed out *my own* application. Wasn't that worthy of some sort of accolade? I came to learn that, according to all standards of "professionalism," it's not. However, each day, many Black teenagers employ the same strategies I did. I argue this is due to a lack of training, education, experience, and mentorship.

In my teenage years, no one sat me down and talked about how to navigate employment. My high school didn't. My father probably dropped some jewels on me, but I don't remember. My friends tried—but they were just as clueless as me.

As a Black teen, navigating workspaces can be daunting, scary, and unfulfilling. Furthermore, most of the world talks about employment as if it is a race-neutral part of society. People act like if you create a high-quality résumé, wear "professional" clothing, interview well, and give a firm handshake, you will automatically get a fair shot at any job you apply to. Unfortunately, this is not only untrue but it can leave you in a false sense of reality. This false sense of reality can make you think that social constructs of race, privilege, and power have no influence on the workforce.

In 1984, researcher and author of *The United-Independent Compensatory Code/System/Concept* Dr. Neely Fuller wrote, "If you do not understand white supremacy/racism, everything you do understand will only confuse you." This quote is especially true for the job market. Your blackness makes you brilliant, resilient, and powerful. Your blackness is also feared and resented by others and may cause them to discriminate against you because of racist notions of Black inferiority that still thrive in America. It is crucial to equip yourself with practical knowledge to help you maneuver through roadblocks and over hurdles that may otherwise steer you away from your employment goals. That is the basis of this book.

This is not your average "how to get a job" guide, the kind you can find in your local workforce development center or bookstore. Those books are typically written from a race-neutral standpoint and lack the cultural relevance and real-world knowledge needed to propel the conversation around Black teen employment. Throughout this book, you will learn about how to confront workplace discrimination, build your talents and skills at a workplace, maintain your cultural identity wherever you choose to work, think long-term about your future, and much more.

Furthermore, this book is not intended to teach you everything there is to know about navigating employment. That would take hundreds if not thousands of pages. This book is designed to be read quickly, possibly in one sitting, so that you can start implementing these strategies ASAP. It is also deliberately structured to allow you to begin reading wherever you feel is best. The information that is not included in this book can be gained by utilizing people and resources around you.

My ask is that you be willing to challenge yourself, take risks, and share this information with your peers. The dominant white culture tells us that everything work-related has to be competitive, individualistic, and exploitative. Yet I contend that in order to achieve whatever opportunity you desire, you must work in unison with others. No one achieves success on their own, though many claim they do. I surely would not have graduated from multiple colleges, become a teacher and youth advocate, and written this book without the continuous support of family, friends, and colleagues.

You are going to achieve many amazing feats in your lifetime. It is ordained within your destiny to be prolific. I hope that by the end of this book, you will be equipped with more tools to add to your toolbelt. Remember that a job is not simply about securing a bag, it is also about gaining skills, knowledge, and opportunities to expand your possibilities in life. Just as you are willing to reap the harvest, you must be willing to plow the land, plant the seeds, and nurture the garden. Now, let us begin.

Part 1

Pre-Employment

CHAPTER 1

Understanding and Challenging Hiring Discrimination

Teen joblessness is a serious problem in America. There are millions of teenagers like you who are seeking professional opportunities but are struggling to land their dream position. In July 2019, the national youth unemployment rate was about 9 percent for teens and young adults ages sixteen to twenty-four, according to the US Bureau of Labor Statistics. The agency also reported this was the lowest unemployment rate for teens and young adults in the last fifty years. However, this number is misleading because it does not include youth unemployment data outside of spring and summer. Year-round the rate is probably much higher, since most youth work more during the spring and summer months. For Black youth, the unemployment rate was higher, hovering around 14 percent. Due to COVID-19 and other factors, youth unemployment (ages sixteen to nineteen) skyrocketed to around 23 percent in June 2020. This means that millions of people your age are not working or earning an income.

If you are a Black teenager, you have surely had a conversation about racism at many points in your life. It may have been after the deaths of Trayvon Martin, Freddie Gray, George Floyd, Breonna Taylor, or Sandra Bland. It may have been after witnessing or being a victim of police brutality while simply living and breathing as a Black person. However, you may not have had a serious conversation about how your race impacts your ability to secure viable employment opportunities.

Let's start by analyzing the horrific reality of hiring discrimination. The US Equal Employment Opportunity Commission (EEOC) prohibits any form of discrimination based on "race, color, religion, sex (including gender identity, sexual orientation, and pregnancy), national origin, age (40 or older), disability or genetic information." These legal protections upheld by the EEOC came to fruition after the Civil Rights Act of 1964 was passed. In the past, racist employers would erect signs literally stating they didn't hire non-whites. Racist slurs and epithets were much more publicly used during the age of your great-grandparents. Now, racism is more covert, and the tactics of hiring discrimination are less obvious and abrupt. You can apply for any position you want, but that does not automatically block employers from discriminating against you based on the aforementioned factors.

The résumé is one of the first places employers begin when unfairly mistreating Black applicants. Research from the Harvard Business School reports that African American applicants who mask or "whiten" the name on their résumé are more likely to get a request to move forward in the application process. This means "Billy" and "Ashley" may get preferential treatment over "Maurice" and "Shaquetta" simply due to their name. This type of discrimination puts Blacks and other non-white job seekers at a massive disadvantage.

Extreme bias can also rear its subtle, inequitable head in the interview. "Where is your family from?" "Are you pregnant, or do you plan to become pregnant in the near future?" "What type of life did you have growing up?" "Are you single or in a relationship?" Believe it or not, all of these extremely inappropriate questions are actually legal, and employers can ask them. Should you take your employer to court, the burden is on you, the employee, to prove that the questions were used to determine your employability, which can be extremely difficult to do. Additionally, you should keep in mind that laws don't prevent people from being immoral. All of the "isms" can be on full display during an interview, so it is important to be aware and have the ability to discern a potential employer's friendly curiosity from a line of inquiry they'll use to unethically eliminate you from the hiring process.

Before we get into some steps you can take to challenge hiring practices that treat Black applicants unfavorably, it is essential for you to understand that most employees who take legal actions to challenge discriminatory practices do not have favorable outcomes. In fact, a 2019 report by the Center for Public Integrity, an investigatory nonprofit, concluded that "workers receive some form of assistance, such as money or a change in work conditions, only 18 percent of the time." The report also noted that claims of racial discrimination "have the lowest success rate."

To Combat These Unjust Hiring Practices, There Are a Few Notable Steps You Can Take:

Document everything: Once you start to believe that you are being discriminated against, you should immediately begin recording your evidence. This can be in a notebook or journal, by using an app on your phone, or you can tell Siri to take notes for you. Documentation is important, because if you move forward with utilizing legal protections, your case will be stronger if you refer to days, times, locations, and other details about the incidences when you were a victim of hiring discrimination.

Consult with an employment lawyer: Employment lawyers provide supportive legal services to employers and employees. They can review your potential case with you and help you weigh the pros and cons of taking legal action against employers, including filing a claim with the EEOC.

File a charge of discrimination: The EEOC has set up a process for filing a charge of discrimination at EEOC. gov. This process involves submitting an online inquiry, scheduling an intake interview, and then filing a charge of discrimination. After a charge of discrimination is filed, the EEOC will begin investigating to collect information about your allegations. If they choose, they may file a lawsuit on your behalf. If they decline to file a lawsuit, you can also do this on your own.

Note: This process can be lengthy and costly, especially if you choose to take your case to court. You should be sure to talk to an employment lawyer and your parents, guardians, mentors, or loved ones before attempting to utilize the services provided by the EEOC.

Contact your state senator: According to researchers and legal experts, one of the reasons why the EEOC is struggling to meet the needs of workers is due to the fact that the agency is underfunded. To help influence funding, you could write your senator and representatives and urge them to advocate for a larger budget for the EEOC. To find out who represents you in Congress, visit gov-track.us and type in your address or select your state.

CHAPTER 2

Stop Playin' About Your Résumé

A résumé is a document used to show someone's vocational and educational background, achievements, and skills. Your résumé is your rep when it comes to employment. For jobs, this is an employer's way of understanding who you are and why they should hire you prior to actually meeting you. Your résumé should be well-written, reviewed, and edited by an experienced professional, and it should highlight the qualities that make you a valuable job candidate. If your résumé is not on point, the likelihood you'll hear back from a job is extremely low.

When I think back to my first job experiences, I wish I had a higher-quality résumé. I wish I took the time to seek assistance from others. My first résumé had grammatical errors and was poorly formatted. If I had asked for help from friends, family members, and others, I am sure it would have helped me become more marketable as a teen job-seeker.

Sally Sad
45 Parents' House Lane, New Britain, CT 06114
(555) 5555-6789 ✉ SALLYBabyGURL@email.com

OBJECTIVE

Awesome graduate of life seeking any fun position requiring a cool girl with a great sense of humor and style!

SUMMARY

- Mostly free, except every day between 2-4 p.m. (gym time)
- Good at holding a converstion about anything
- Great at updating Facebook and anything I can post pictures on

EDUCATION

Central Connecticut City High School, New Britain, CT
High School Diploma

WORK EXPERIENCE

High School Yearbook, New Britain, CT
Photographer (Setpember 2006-June 2007)

- Shot pics of my friends!
- Added cute details in Photoshop
- Went to weekly meetings

First Job Burgers, Wallingford, CT
Grill Cook (September 2007-Present)

- Flip burgers and fill condiment containers
- Deal with annoying costumer requests
- Answer phone

Bakery Best, New Britain, CT
Volunteer Cupcake Tester (June 2006-August 2006)

- Liked chocolate best

HOBBIES

Dancing, Photography, Social Media

Poor-quality résumé from EducationWorld.com

As you can see, this poor-quality résumé has multiple typos, an unprofessional email address, and even an image in the top-right corner. This résumé needs some love and attention. It is essential to have someone else thoroughly read over your résumé and offer you sound advice prior to submitting it to an employer. Even with me writing this book, I leaned heavily on an editor and went through various stages of editing and development before providing you the book you are reading right now.

Joe Graduate
123 First Apartment Ave., Hartford, CT 06114
(555) 555-1234 📧 JoeGraduate@email.com

OBJECTIVE
Ambitious and creative recent graduate seeks a challenging position that requires exceptional writing, editing, comprehension and interpersonal skills.

SUMMARY
- Flexible; can adjust quickly to any setting
- Excels at tasks requiring communication skills
- Adept with complex data platforms
- Proficient in Microsoft Word, Excel and PowerPoint

EDUCATION
Great Connecticut State University, New Britain, CT
B.A. in English with minor in journalism (Sept. 2005-May 2009)

RELATED COURSES

Editing	Feature Story Writing
Qualitative Analysis	Page Design

WORK EXPERIENCE
Hartford Community Newspaper Hartford, CT
Freelance Writer (August 2009-Present)
- Writes multiple daily stories on a variety of topics
- Shoots photographs to serve as art for own stories
- Coordinates deadlines and task schedules with editors
- Participates in weekly productivity meetings

Student TV Station, New Britain, CT
Copy Editor (September 2008-June 2009)
- Edited all on-air content copy
- Brainstormed daily content with staff writers
- Managed writing staff before/after daily morning show
- Managed office inventory

First Job Burgers, Wallingford, CT
Shift Leader (June 2006-August 2007)
- Maintained a clean, orderly and well-stocked restaurant
- Provided impeccable service at front counter and drive-thru
- Managed all staff and ensured high performance and efficiency

VOLUNTEER

American Disease Society	Event Volunteer (2004-Present)
Camp Rising Moon	Summer Painting Instructor (2004, 2005)

High-quality high school résumé from EducationWorld.com

As you can see in this example, Joe was able to produce a higher-quality résumé by choosing his words carefully, strongly describing his experience, and providing a more professional email address. Joe's résumé could have been enhanced by removing the computer image, but this résumé would resonate with an employer much more than the one produced by Sally.

Over time, through independent research on Google and by asking questions, I made my résumé stronger. In this day and age, you can find the answer to almost any question in seconds through an online search. There are a ton of free résumé-building websites on the internet. Your local library would also be a great way to start exploring résumé creation. If possible, I would suggest seeking out a trained professional to support you. For example, in February 2020, I found résumé writer and career coach Charmanique Anderson on Instagram. After reviewing her work and seeing her client testimonials, I decided to purchase her résumé support services in order to drastically improve the structure and content of my résumé. She did a superb job and was extremely thorough. Immediately after submitting my newly polished résumé, I got two interview requests. It's important that you take advantage of this digital age we are living in by using technology to your professional advantage. As the title of this chapter says, stop playin' about your résumé!

Tips to Improve the Quality of Your Résumé:

Be sure to highlight your volunteer experiences: This can include community service, mentoring, tutoring, cleaning up trash, and beautifying your neighborhood.

Include any entrepreneurial experience you have: This includes mowing lawns, selling waters, shoveling snow, and taking care of a neighbor's pet. These tasks may seem menial, but for your first résumé, they could make a huge difference.

Take your time crafting your objective or summary, and make sure it connects to the job you are applying for: You can see an example of this in Joe's résumé. He outlines who he is—a professional—and what type of employment opportunity he is seeking. This section may require some practice, but if written well, it helps employers gain a greater sense of who you are, what you are seeking, and what value you bring to the job.

ALWAYS ask for help when you need it: This résumé support can come by way of your teachers, guidance counselor, mentors, coaches, parents/guardians, and people who work at local job centers. You would be surprised at how much joy your network will find in supporting you. Though it might take some time to ask for and incorporate their feedback, this will pay off in the long run.

Visit your local library: Public libraries offer so much great community-centered programming that's overlooked and undervalued. You should go visit the one that is closest to you and take some time to talk to the staff about creating a résumé. They may be able to point you in the direction of free resources and workshops to assist you.

CHAPTER 3

Create a Simple, Professional Email Address

In 2004, AIM, an instant messenger program created by America Online, was one of my generation's first social networking experiences on the internet. I remember talking to multiple girls (probably at the same time) on this platform. My friends and I also connected on it—long before Facebook, Instagram, and TikTok. I think my username was "lorshoty" or something like that. I actually spelled the word *short* wrong (unintentionally) and just left it that way. For those who don't know, *lor* is another way of saying *little*. One of my late friends, Eddie, had a wilder username than me. I think it was due to all the Three 6 Mafia we listened to back in those days. He went by "BodySnatcha04." He never killed anybody or "snatched" any bodies, but it sounded cool, so he ran with it.

You may have a dope username you use on social media, too, and maybe you also use it as part of your email address.

Something like "ThatGuy123" is pretty innocent and nonabrasive. However, in the current work climate, recruiters and hiring managers are not looking for creativity when reviewing résumés. You don't get any bonus points for describing your personality, hobbies, or favorite colors within your email address. It's best to keep it simple and use variations of your first and last name combined with some numbers, dashes, or periods.

For example, if my name were Maurice Thomas, the following email addresses would work well:
MauriceThomas@imail.com
Maurice.Thomas@imail.com
MauriceThomas123@imail.com

You should keep in mind that your first-choice username may already be taken. You should think of two or three options as backups. The difference between ThatGuy123@gmail.com and Maurice.Thomas@gmail.com is a potential interview request and a résumé that ends up in the trash can, like my Foot Locker one probably did. #Kobe

CHAPTER 4

Let's Talk Social Media

For years, we've heard that we should "do it for the gram" in order to gain social media followers and attention. However, when searching for a job, you need to consider the content you're putting out there, even if you have a private social media account. In 2017, a CareerBuilder survey found that 70 percent of employers use social media to screen candidates before hiring them. This means there is a very good chance that anything you post, whether positive or negative, will be seen by a job you are applying for. Unfortunately, some jobs will immediately deem you unfit for an interview, simply by looking through your IG stories or TikTok videos. You should take some necessary steps to ensure your social media persona reflects what you want employers to know about you.

Ways to Get Your Social Media on Point:

Delete some stuff: I encourage you to delete any posts that show or discuss weapons, drugs, violence, sex, or illegal activities. Unless you are posting about a historical event, like Nat Turner's rebellion, or sharing some sort of article or critique, you may want to remove any graphic content. You also do not want to run the risk of incriminating yourself. Police departments monitor social media way more than you think.

Deactivate or delete old, unmonitored accounts: Do you have an older Twitter account you created three years ago but never use? Delete it. Did you start making an Instagram page but not get around to finishing it? Delete that, too. You need to be knowledgeable of any accounts that represent you or your likeness. You are a brand, and you should treat yourself that way.

Change your bio to show your professional aspirations: Even if your page is private, an employer may be able to see the information in your bio. That small bit of information can have an astronomical impact on your chances of getting an interview request. Remember: any content that is public-facing should represent the best version of yourself. I recommend including your professional aspirations in your bio. This way, employers and other nosy people can see your goals. Additionally, the more you think, talk, and act in alignment with your goals, the more likely you are to achieve them. Check out a book called *The Secret* to learn more about this concept.

Follow the social media accounts of companies you want to work for: If you want to become a basketball player, you should be following players, coaches, trainers, owners, and other important folks who are a part of the sports industry. The same goes for any other job or career you are interested in. You can learn a lot about a person or company by monitoring their posts. You can see what their passions are, what hobbies they love, and the type of people that work with and for them.

Avoid using profanity while job searching: Listen, we all curse. It is not new. My advice here is that if you would not say it in a church or in front of your grandparents, try to keep it off social media, especially if it has no real context or deeper meaning.

If you are sixteen or over, join LinkedIn: Beyond Facebook, Instagram, and Snapchat, there are other social media networks you should join. One of them is LinkedIn. I first learned about LinkedIn as a college student at Morgan State University. My professors urged my classmates and me to join. At the time, I was a die-hard journalist and young professional. LinkedIn showcased my professional experiences and skills, and gave me direct access to industry professionals. Instead of working to find an employer's contact information, I could contact recruiters directly and inquire about job opportunities. I encourage you to also join this social media platform.

CHAPTER 5

The Untold Story of "Professional Dress"

I have a secret to tell you. This is something that many employment guides will not reveal to you because it steers the conversation around employment to an uncomfortable space for some. However, I want you to be clear on "professional dress" standards in the workplace. These standards were created by white culture. Now, do not get me wrong, workplace dress varies depending on the type of industry you work in. For example, lawyers typically wear suits, while millennial computer programmers go to work in T-shirts and jeans. However, white people have a major hand in determining American dress standards.

According to *The Atlantic*, the start-up culture in Silicon Valley—a majority-white technology and innovation hub in Northern California—had a major influence on the shift in "professional" attire in the 1990s. Before this time, "dress-down" days and "casual Fridays" were not widely accepted in the business world. The universal workplace standard, for the most part, was a suit or something similar. However, as companies began to focus more on individual innovation instead of a rigid, cookie-cutter look, their dress standards changed.

Because white people have the majority cultural influence in determining American professional dress standards, non-white people are often discriminated against when they appear outside of the "norm." This makes clothing like dashikis, commonly worn by people of African descent, outside of the expectation. American standards of professional dress also deem clothing commonly worn by teenagers as "streetwear." This means your ripped jeans, tank tops, open-toe shoes, jerseys, and T-shirts are not seen as workplace-appropriate in most cases. Tattoos, piercings, bright hair colors, and even natural hair, like afros and locs, are considered unprofessional in the eyes of many employers.

Did you know that in 2019, California had to pass the Create a Respectful and Open Workplace for Natural Hair (CROWN) Act to protect Black people from being discriminated against by employers upholding anti-blackness in American work culture? In my hometown of Baltimore, a Black woman named Farryn Johnson was awarded $250,000 in 2015 because she was a target of racial discrimination at a Hooters restaurant. A manager did not approve of the highlights in her hair and reportedly told her, "Black people don't have blonde hair." This is another reason we can't pretend like workforce development is race-neutral.

The societal standards of professionalism are important to keep in mind as you begin to search for an employment opportunity. As biased as the standards are, you want to be knowledgeable of them. You want to know them not just to gain an employment opportunity but to strategize about how you can challenge and eliminate unjust job practices. See chapter 8 for more about on-the-job discrimination and some ideas about what you should know and do if you're discriminated against while working.

CHAPTER 6

Applying for Opportunities

The ability to successfully apply to opportunities is a basic function that helps separate interested opportunity seekers from actual applicants in the pipeline to be connected to employment. Applications can be long, boring, redundant, and even intimidating. Employers and other opportunity holders do not always think enough about what it's like to be on the receiving end of the applications they produce. The language can be uninviting, and the amount of time it takes to complete applications should be illegal in some cases. However, as an opportunity seeker, you want to be tedious, relentless, and enduring when completing applications.

I contend that online job applications usually suck. I remember laughing with my friends as a teenager about how jobs ask you to upload your résumé AND THEN fill in every aspect of your job history—the same job history you included in your résumé! To this day, this still annoys me! While it may not be worth your while to complain to an employer about their application process, it's worth learning how to submit a superb application, which can help the application process go more quickly and lead to greater success.

Here Are Some Tips for Success:

Be concise with your words: In life, many of us have a tendency to talk—a lot. Sometimes this can be rewarding, and the way we elaborate can be seen as impressive. In other cases, especially on an application, you want to get your point across without wordiness and rambling. For example, instead of describing yourself as "a person who is trustworthy," you could say "a trustworthy person."

Double-check your work: Like your teacher always tells you before turning in an assignment, you should always make sure to check your work for accuracy and completeness prior to hitting the submit button. There's nothing worse than forgetting to complete a question or not spelling a word correctly, knowing your work is going to be reviewed by someone in HR.

Seek help when needed: I encourage you to ask a mentor, teacher, friend, or an employed adult to check over your application before you complete and submit it. They may see mistakes that you've missed and be able to offer you feedback to increase your chances of obtaining an opportunity. Your network is all around you waiting to support you—use it!

CHAPTER 7

Prepare for Your Interview

Admittedly, I have exceptional interviewing skills. If I had to guess, it probably came from doing a considerable amount of public speaking while in high school. As a member of a Baltimore-based, Pan-African organization, Solvivaz Nation, I occasionally spoke during lectures and workshops to help intro the event to guests. I also did some emceeing as a teenager. No—really. I was in a group of about seven artists known as Sunz of New Afrikan Teachers (N.A.T.). We were like the younger, Black nationalist version of Wu-Tang Clan. Through rapping in the studio, performing in front of audiences, and watching others, I honed my presence as an orator.

But if you're getting ready for your first interview and you don't have a ton of speaking experience, don't worry. If you google "how to interview," you will find a plethora of resources that can help you improve your craft. To me, the key to interviewing successfully is knowing your audience and adapting your delivery and content to fit the folks in the room. For example, while interviewing for a school administrator position, I made sure to talk heavily about my work in education and with young people.

I infused joy and laughter into the conversation, along with personal stories and professional outcomes. I read my interviewer like a book. He nodded, laughed, and smirked right along with me. That let me know that I had him on my fishing line—he was fully immersed in our dialogue.

In contrast, when I interviewed for a job at Walden University, I spoke about the way I coached adults and supported them as professionals. This was more of what the role entailed and what the interviewer was looking to learn about me. I was not offered a position with this institution—probably due to the fact that the office was as white as a snowstorm in Alaska, but I still think my interview was stellar. The two women I interviewed with also informed me of my talent in this area.

There are many ways to interview, but it's imperative that you are relaxed and in control of your self-presentation, which includes how you move, your tone of voice, and your overall body language. You should use your intuition to understand the moment and embrace it. If you bomb on a question, own it. Then, think about how you can improve on the next one. If you need a few moments to ponder before answering a question, make it known and utilize that time to formulate your thoughts. While interviewing, remember that you are an asset and that your job is to bring your résumé to life. You should have stories loaded up in your mind that you've rehearsed and are ready to deliver. Lastly, be sure you feel comfortable talking about areas of work where you struggled and overcame adversity. This will not only show your humanness, but this also demonstrates your ability to be vulnerable, reflective, and solutions-oriented.

To Improve Your Interviewing Abilities:

Practice a LOT: They say proper preparation prevents poor performance. This saying is especially true for interviewing. You get better at it by practicing, getting feedback, and making tweaks as you go. To practice on your own, I recommend looking at yourself in the mirror. You should see yourself as you are talking. You should hear yourself and look at how you move and how your voice changes as you speak. In essence, you want to see what an employer sees when they interview you. Is your voice cracking, or are you extra fidgety due to your nervousness? Are you too loud? Is it hard to hear yourself?

If you practice with a partner, you can get constructive feedback from someone you know and trust that can help you take your skills to the next level. I am sure a family member or friend would be down to support you. You can also reverse roles and become the person who provides the feedback. The learning process and feedback loop is never-ending.

Again, use the resources around you: There are so many interview skill-building supports online. You can literally type "interview skills" into a search engine and get some quality information. You should not have to spend a dime to get top-notch interview advice. Take some time to do some searching and internalizing.

Prepare follow-up questions: No matter where you interview, you should always have a few follow-up questions to ask your interviewers at the end. A good rule of thumb is to have at least five questions on-hand. Why five? Well, from my experience, I have learned that one or two questions you have may be answered by the interviewer before you get a chance to ask them. You don't want that to be the reason you have no questions.

Some possible follow-up questions include:

- What are the next steps in the interview process, and when can I expect to hear from you?
- What are some of the company's goals within the next few years?
- How did the company support staff and other members of the organization before, during, and after the COVID-19 pandemic?
- What is the typical career path for someone starting in my role?
- What does a day in the role look like?

Listen carefully: When interviewing, you want to be a strong, active listener. You should try your best to remember the names and roles of people you are interviewing with, along with how their work connects to the position you are interviewing for. There may also be other helpful information to be attentive to. As you listen, feel free to take notes.

Know the company: Before applying to any job, you should do some preliminary research on the company and find out what they are about. This can include, but is not limited to, visiting their website, watching videos related to the company, looking at any news associated with the company, and checking to see if you know anyone who works there or has worked there in the past. After getting an interview request, your research should increase. You should look into the person who will be interviewing you and work to have a solid understanding of the role you are interviewing for.

You should know the answer to questions like:

- What does the company do?
- What services do they provide?
- What are they known for?
- Have they been in the news for anything controversial?

Send a thank-you note to the interviewer: For most of my teenage years, I did not do this. However, I would now consider this step essential. After you interview, you should always follow up with an email or written letter thanking the people you interviewed with. This thoughtful gesture is not guaranteed to get you a job, but it does show gratitude.

Part 2

Maintaining and Making the Most of Employment

CHAPTER 8

On-the-Job Discrimination

According to the EEOC, as mentioned in the first part of this book, racial discrimination in the workplace is illegal. We focused on hiring discrimination in the first part of the book, but on-the-job discrimination is also a hellacious problem for job seekers of color, especially Black ones. These forms of discrimination can be indirect and unintentional, but their impact remains highly detrimental.

Discrimination can be demonstrated in various ways, including:

- Women with equivalent credentials and experience to men being paid less than men for the same type of work.
- Policies and practices that target natural hairstyles regularly worn by Black employees, including braids, afros, and locs.
- Teenagers losing shifts or being unfairly denied leave, benefits, or other rights and amenities legally provided to them.

In your lifetime, you may experience various forms of discrimination due to your age, race, socioeconomic status, gender identification, national origin, disability, and professional experience. Many employers may not value your blackness and youthfulness and may see you as a detriment to or insignificant part of their companies. This is something to keep in mind and be prepared for.

When I was fourteen, my first job experience was through YouthWorks, a summer youth employment program in Baltimore. I worked as a camp counselor at Harlem Park Recreation Center in West Baltimore. Each year, tens of thousands of Baltimore youth apply for this summer employment opportunity, but thousands do not land jobs, so I was elated to be hired during the summer of 2004. Unfortunately, as I reflect back on my experience as a young worker, I feel I was a victim of gender-based discrimination that's illegal under federal employment discrimination laws, as well as state and local statutes.

I still remember the experience as clear as day. I was walking to the bathroom and overheard my supervisor, a Black man, ask a co-worker of mine, a Black girl, to mop the floor. She laughed off the request, refused to do the task, and walked away. My supervisor, not knowing I had overheard the exchange, saw me walking in his direction and asked me to do the task my co-worker had just declined. I was disgusted that he even asked me to do the task and told him that I was not going to do it, either. He had a reputation for allowing the girls at our site to get away with not fulfilling their job duties while urging the guys to "pick up the slack." I am not sure what his reason for this was—maybe he grew up in a household where men were expected to do more physical work, or maybe he was this way because none of the other guys stood up to him and questioned his ways. All I knew was, I wasn't having it! He gave me two choices: I could either clean the floor or go home, so I decided to stick to my morals, and I left work for the day.

I came back to work the next day, and business continued as usual. I did not know any formal process to rectify my issues, and I don't even think I told my parents. I guess I just thought this was the way things were supposed to be. I did not know that I had legal protections that could support me. If this happened in 2020, I could reach out to Baltimore's Office of Equity and Civil Rights, the Maryland Commission on Civil Rights, and the EEOC to gather information on the appropriate actions to take. In May 2020, I described my situation to a lawyer who used to work for the EEOC, and he told me, "It is possible that what you described could have been considered discrimination, but you would need to prove a clear pattern and intent and tie those things into state and federal law during that time." Even if I did know how to advocate for myself at that age, I probably would not have taken the time to voice my concerns and seek advice. Thus, I allowed myself to lose pay and became a victim of possibly illegal gender-based discrimination.

The scenario I just described is nothing special or out of the ordinary. It happens every day in America. Most of the time it's not challenged or reported. Most employees suffer in silence out of fear of losing their job or suffering other forms of retaliation from employers. I pray you avoid this reality, and here are some tools to do just that.

Here Are Some Ways You Can Resist:

Ask your employer if your job is racially equitable: When you feel comfortable enough and have done your research, ask your employer how they are working to make your workplace racially equitable. Specifically, inquire about how they are supporting Black youth like you and ensuring you thrive in the workplace instead of merely existing.

Take notes: If you feel like you are encountering issues related to the workplace, take these concerns to your union, HR department, or support group to think through how to generate solutions to your concerns.

Watch **The Spook Who Sat by the Door***:* This movie is the fictional story of the first Black CIA officer. It shows how you can infiltrate an organization, absorb information, and use it to empower your community while challenging oppression.

Connect with like-minded employees: It's imperative to network with people at your job to talk and work through proposals and other suggestions to improve the quality of your workplace. There is power in numbers.

Refer to suggestions from the hiring discrimination chapter: You may need to contact the EEOC, HR department, or even secure a lawyer. All of your potential options should be weighed and considered when challenging workplace discrimination.

Note: Most companies are resistant to deep, structural changes and operate as if they have cracked the code on being equitable. These strategies for resistance can isolate you from some of your co-workers and could potentially lead to your termination. I would be grossly misleading you if I did not mention this information to you now. Before making a decision or moving on an action, talk with your mentors, loved ones, and people you trust in order to weigh the pros and cons.

CHAPTER 9

Become Knowledgeable of Human Resources

During the beginning of your tenure at any job, you will come into contact with the human resources department or the person who serves this role. Human resources makes sure staff are well supported and protected. They typically shepherd you through filling out new employee paperwork and provide you with a handbook that details the ins and outs of your workplace. Additionally, they should be able to advise you on how to report a grievance and take advantage of benefits and incentives associated with your job. The quality of HR can vary from one company to the next, and smaller companies may not have an HR department at all.

The US Department of Labor legally protects employees at the federal level. States vary on protections offered to employees. However, employers often count on employees to know their legal rights. After you've been informed once by your employer, you may not be reminded about your rights without requesting more information. Being unaware of your legal protections can be dangerous. If you are unaware of your rights, you could potentially be mistreated without even knowing it. Before you accept any job, be clear on your wage, the taxes that will be taken from your pay, your job description and responsibilities, and the hours you are expected to work. As an employee, make sure you have everything in writing. If you rely on word of mouth alone, things may change or get confusing. By having things in writing, you can help to better protect yourself against exploitation.

Companies pride themselves on being "diverse" and "equal opportunity employers," yet some demonize Black culture and severely limit the opportunities afforded to Black youth. At work, start to notice if the eloquent mission and vision statements posted on a company website match their daily practices and policies. I say this not to scare you, but to encourage you to think critically in the workplace and to ask questions when needed. As a teacher told me years ago, "The only stupid question is the one you don't ask." Do you have questions about your pay? Ask HR. Do you have concerns about something written in your contract or some other document you are required to sign? Ask HR. Do you need an additional copy of a form? Ask HR. They literally exist to support you.

To Learn More about What HR Can Do for You:

Shadow someone who works in HR: If you have some time, see if you can coordinate with your supervisor and someone in HR to set up a shadow experience. They may not be able to show you everything due to confidentiality, but they can show you some of what they do and how it benefits you and other members of the company.

Join HR-facilitated gatherings: Mandatory all-staff trainings and meetings are, well, mandatory. Other times, you may have the option to attend learning sessions. After coordinating with your supervisor, you should work to attend these trainings to bolster your understanding of HR and generally learn new information about how HR functions. Additionally, these trainings can help you learn professional skills.

Career support: Looking to get a college degree or grow professionally in order to get a different position within your company? Well, HR can support here as well. They may be able to alert you to trainings, programs, and institutions to help further your professional aspirations.

CHAPTER 10

Know How You Will Be Evaluated

Man, I wish I learned about this when I was a teenager. I wish someone had told me to think about metrics and performance measures in order to be the best employee I can be. Young person, wherever you are in the world reading this book, I want you to lock in on this section, because you may never see it written about in any other workforce development guide for teens—or even adults, for that matter.

Metrics are the standards by which you will be measured as a professional in your role. You should know them and internalize them before beginning any employment opportunity. Performance metrics can look different depending on where you work and what your job requires. For example, professional running backs know they are required to run certain routes, master play calls and routines, and provide other contributions to their football team. They know this before the first snap of the first game. Before they get evaluated, they should have had a conversation with their coaches and trainers about what they will be expected to do.

When I was nineteen, I worked as a sales associate at For Your Entertainment (FYE), a chain entertainment retail store, in Mondawmin Mall. For context, Mondawmin is located in West Baltimore and is the only mall in Baltimore. My job was to stock shelves, help customers check out, provide customer service, and—unbeknownst to me—serve as a top-secret security guard to make sure people were not stealing the store's merchandise. The job was simple and allowed me to make some steady income while I was studying at Baltimore City Community College, right up the street.

While there, sales was the name of the game. Both of my managers wanted me and other sales associates to sell like we were going out of business (which actually did end up happening, shortly after I resigned). To entice customers to buy, we tried to bundle items together as a form of upselling. For instance, if someone was buying a TLC album, I would also encourage them to check out the discounted R&B section, or if the customer was getting a Young Jeezy album, I might also encourage them to check out other new hip-hop music that just dropped. The goal was to average at least three units per ticket for each customer. Basically, we wanted each customer to buy three or more items. That was the most important metric in my position.

I became an upselling monster. My performance was so good that I got promoted to key holder, which meant I could open and close the store and deposit money into the bank at the end of the day. I also got a raise in pay and had managerial responsibilities if my supervisor was out. At one point, I was second in the district in sales, too. In my mind, I was the Marshawn Lynch of sales. #BeastMode. This success came only after becoming deeply entrenched in learning and homing in on the art of selling the items in my store. I studied my managers and took what they taught me and added my own flavor to it. I probably made FYE a lot of money, too.

Before starting your job, you need to ask your potential employer about how your work performance will be evaluated. This will allow you to see how you are performing. Specifically, you will be able to determine if you are meeting your individual performance goals or not. By consistently performing above the metrics your employer uses to determine your success on your evaluations, you could renegotiate your job terms and make an argument for higher pay, a new position, different hours, and other incentives. You should inquire with your job about how frequently you will be formally evaluated. The goal should always be to execute at a high level in whatever you do.

CHAPTER 11

Preserve Your Cultural Identity at Work

Culture is the knowledge, customs, characteristics, and manifestations of a people. Your culture is who you are on the inside and out. It is the way you dress, talk, pray, sleep, sing, eat, and ultimately be who you are. You should appreciate and embody your culture, because without it, you are living someone else's reality. In the workplace, it is important to maintain your culture. Each job has a unique work culture—a way they operate and expect you to operate. However, beneath those rules and practices, there is an underlying and often hidden culture that can overrule your own culture if you allow it.

Just as developers gentrify poor Black neighborhoods, our cultures can also be gentrified, and our heritage can be shelved for that of another cultural group. As a Black teenager, you have to remember that your intellect, customs, and identity are valuable. No work culture, be it dominated by whites or another group of people, should define for you what your blackness should look, feel, or sound like. You don't have to put raisins in your potato salad just because Susie from your job said it tastes better that way. You also should not force yourself to laugh at offensive jokes or alienate yourself from other Black or Brown people in order to appease white people.

Your culture adds value to who you are as an employee. You have knowledge, skills, and other attributes that your co-workers may not have. Your grasp on blackness is authentic and makes you powerful, resilient, resourceful, and innovative. For example, if you have lived in poverty, you may have had to create a basketball hoop from empty plastic crates because you did not have access to an adequate basketball court. Additionally, because you are living in a digital age, you may be tech-savvy and knowledgeable of apps and computer programs that are foreign to your co-workers. Regardless of where your professional journey takes you, your culture should remain by your side like white on rice, as elders say.

Here Are Some Ways to Maintain Your Culture in the Workplace:

Don't just listen; share your experiences as well: You were not born to simply listen and absorb. Your words matter, and you should share them, especially when you feel like you can add value to the discussion.

Be mindful of and respond to what people say about Black people: Black people are not monolithic. We do not all talk, think, act, and exist in the same way. Sure, there are many similarities between one Black person and the next, but the experiences of a Black person in one city or town can be vastly different from those of someone living in a different area. So, when you hear Black people being generalized into one homogenous bucket, be sure to correct the speaker—even if the speaker is you. #ProtectTheCulture

Be comfortable with standing out: I am sure someone has told you to be original and to not follow the trends others set. However, most people are comfortable following others because it reduces the spotlight on them. It is scary to be different. Yet, I encourage you to separate yourself from mediocrity. Mediocrity can come in the form of people or even thoughts that can deter you from being your best self. For example, if you are constantly pessimistic, you may need to adjust your mindset to embrace optimism.

CHAPTER 12

Keep Developing Your Skills

Most young people I know are not aware of the valuable skills, certifications, experiences, and other résumé boosters you can gain from a job. For example, being a cashier at a restaurant can lead to the acquisition of transferrable skills. You are learning how to directly interact with customers, use various forms of technology, and deal with commerce. These are all important, transferrable, and marketable skills.

You can gain free certifications and trainings simply by working at a particular place. For example, when I was an AmeriCorps Community Service-Learning Fellow at The Choice Program, I earned a ServSafe certification, which proved I was able to safely manage food products. I also completed a Crisis Prevention Institute training that equipped me with skills and a certificate that showed that I could nonviolently defuse volatile situations. These certifications are valued at hundreds of dollars, and I obtained them for free. I also was able to use them as résumé boosters when I applied for other jobs.

Wherever you work, you should look for opportunities to obtain free trainings, certifications, experiences, and other résumé boosters. Doing so could entail all-expenses paid trips. I was able to go to Tampa, Memphis, and Montgomery—all through work. While I attended Baltimore City Community College in 2009, I traveled to Italy for three weeks—again, for free—as a part of the Granville T. Woods Scholars Program. A friend of mine is an Information Technology (IT) professional, and he travels to Amsterdam a few times per year to complete work assignments. When traveling, his flight, hotel, food, and fees are all paid for. As a young employee, you should always seek chances to advance, learn, and grow. In the long run, this will help distinguish you.

CHAPTER 13

Think Strategically about Your Paper

I wish I could get back all the money I wasted at check-cashing spots. I wish I would have scaled back on purchasing so many clothes. I wish I didn't spend $600 on a light-blue 1986 Buick LeSabre from a Pennsylvania auction that only lasted me a few months. Like many adults will tell you, you should be mindful of your money habits. However, most adults in America struggle with finances. According to a 2013 Gallup poll, only about 30 percent of Americans have a detailed budget, and roughly 50 percent of Americans live paycheck to paycheck. My hope is that you will be in a better financial circumstance.

Before you make your mark with an employer, you should think about your budget. A budget is essentially a financial plan. It helps you outline where your money goes and how much of it goes where. This is easier to do before you have bills and other financial obligations because none of your money has a predetermined purpose or destination. Regardless of where you are on your journey, you should think about some smart ways to manage your income.

In your budget, you should allow for savings. This is money you put into a bank account, safe, top-secret vault, or anyplace that's extremely secure. Most financial experts will tell you to put at least 10 percent of your income into a savings account. Depending on your goals and financial obligations, you may even be able to save more. When I was a teenager, I undervalued saving. My intention was to make my income stretch for fourteen days—until my next check came and I was able to repeat this paycheck-to-paycheck lifestyle. If you are wiser with your finances as a teenager, you will hopefully develop into a stronger money manager than I was.

Another important part of your budget is your bills. From a cell phone and rent to a car payment and utility bill, chances are you have or will soon have some sort of bill you are responsible for paying on a monthly basis. To ensure that these bills are paid on time, I recommend setting up automatic payments or scheduling time each month to manually pay your bills. This way, you can avoid late fees and assure that you have not forgotten to pay a bill. In addition to just paying bills, be wise about how many bills you accrue. Think about the basics—food, clothes, shelter, childcare, and other essential needs—before you decide to make frivolous purchases or get a credit card or cable television.

To Recap, Make Sure You Do the Following ASAP:

- Establish a budget
- Figure out a way to securely save your money
- Take a critical look at your bills or any bills you want to establish
- Be wise about your spending

CHAPTER 14

Managing Workplace Stress

Stress kills, bruh. Stress kills, sis. Stress can weaken your immune system, damage your organs, and cause you to age faster. Black might not crack, but stress will have you looking a mess. Across the country, and even in other parts of the world, people cite jobs as a major stressor. From annoying supervisors to barely livable wages, your workplace can cause you a tremendous amount of stress.

One of the most stressful occupations I ever had was working in a struggling school. There was high turnover in leadership, the culture of the school was fight or flight—and there wasn't much fleeing going on—and the founder of the school was incompetent and highly condescending. He was the type of guy to smile in your face and then start criticizing you once you were a few feet away.

Working in this school environment wore on my soul and physical well-being. I vividly remember going home and feeling like I had just left a sparring match at a boxing gym. My body ached, my head pounded, and my feet hurt. I was the definition of exhausted. I felt depleted of all the joy I once had when interviewing and getting established in my role. That good, wholesome feeling of joy was replaced with despair and frustration. On top of that, I heard rumors that the school was in danger of closing and being investigated by Baltimore City Public Schools for poor management and excessive complaints from parents. Needless to say, I had to make a move to maintain my sanity. I ended up resigning from this position mid-school year. It was a tough decision to make. I left before I had a new job lined up, which I would urge you not to do unless you can afford it and have determined there are no other options.

After some reflection and eventually getting a new job, I realized then, and even to this day, that I need to do better with my stress management. It is a daily process I am working to improve on in order to change habits and build healthier routines. While there are many ways you can reduce stress in the workplace, here are a few I have learned in my employment journey.

Aromatherapy: Used for centuries, aromatherapy involves the inhalation of vaporized essential oils that have been diluted by water. These water vapors are created inside of an aroma diffuser that you can get from a local health store or a popular retailer in your area. When stressed, you can put a few drops of lavender or peppermint oil into your aroma diffuser with about a cup of water, and then let that baby work its magic! Within a few seconds, you will be breathing in a healthy dose of molecules that have been linked to stress reduction, improved respiratory function, and lower blood pressure.

Plants: As a child, I remember elders talking to plants. They would greet them, thank them, and engage with them often. I thought those were strange practices then, but now I realize how important plants are. At my desk right now, there is a neon pothos plant that brings me the greatest joy. These plants purify the air, help eliminate odors, and assist me with keeping my calm in the workplace. Keep a plant on your desk if you have one. If this is not possible, travel outside during the workday and spend some time next to trees or even in the grass. If you want some extra earthiness, place your bare feet in the grass and close your eyes for a few seconds.

Deep breaths: Through yoga and mindfulness, I've gained a deep appreciation for the power of breathing. Most of us breathe because it's an involuntary bodily function, but you should learn to appreciate your breath. According to a 2015 *Harvard Health* article, deep breathing can "slow the heartbeat and lower or stabilize blood pressure." High blood pressure is a major risk factor for a variety of diseases and other health conditions. When feeling stressed due to work, try to find some time to close your eyes and breathe for a few moments.

Have a conversation with your supervisor: In an ideal world, your supervisor should be your biggest champion in the workplace. Why? Because if you are managing your stress well, chances are you will be your most productive self at work. I encourage you to express to your supervisor how you feel to gather some advice. If your supervisor sucks and lacks the moral decency to support you as a human being, feel free to look for others at your workplace to confide in if you feel comfortable. If not, check in with HR to ask about what supports are offered to you through your Employee Assistance Program (EAP). You can also seek support from your health insurance company.

Ask Granny for advice: Our grandparents hold some of the most pertinent wisdom known to humankind. It's important to talk with all members of your family, including your parents or guardians, but grandparents often have those parables and allegories to help you make sense of your situation. This would be a good time to go sit down at the feet of your elder and request support.

Resign if needed: While I don't recommend it as a first resort, sometimes resigning and transitioning to another job is the best option. Before moving on this option, you should try some of the other aforementioned recommendations. You'll learn more about the resignation process in the next part of the book.

CHAPTER 15

Be Willing to Learn from Others

"The more you know, the more you learn that you don't know." I couldn't tell you who taught me that saying, but somewhere along the road of life, that saying stuck in my brain. It basically means that there is no end of learning. There will never be a point in time where you have mastered all there is and no longer need to gain knowledge from others. Often, people who feel like they have reached the pinnacle of knowledge miss critical information that could take them to the next level. My dad once told me, "Son, I don't want you to be like me. I want you to be better than me." That is the same way I think about the youth of today.

Each day provides a new opportunity to learn from others. At each job you have, there will be some key staff members who can "put you on game," as they say. It could be the custodian, who is probably underpaid and worked to death. I find that these folks are usually some of the wisest in the buildings where I have worked. They have seen a lot and are masters of being resourceful. I have learned a lot about being consistent and timely from these folks.

When I was Lower School Dean of Culture at Baltimore Collegiate School for Boys, two of my supervisors, Dr. Kelli Seaton and Mr. Makael Burrell, helped me sharpen my presentation skills by showing me how to infuse data and practical engagement strategies. Although things did not work out at the school, I'm still blessed to have been able to learn from these two education professionals.

While I was teaching at Southwest Baltimore Charter School, Mr. Corey Gaber, Mrs. Gena Proctor, and Mr. Geoff Godfrey were godsends when it came to content and pedagogy. To learn how to build better relationships with my students, I studied the ways of Mr. Tee Carroll and learned a ton from fellow educators and educational resources.

The people around you are invaluable. Be strategic in how you utilize people and how you allow others to utilize you.

To Learn from Others, You Should:

Engage people: Sometimes we can be so "cool" that we block blessings that are right in front of us. If there is someone you want to learn something from, let them know. Be upfront about it. As they say, "A closed mouth don't get fed."

Practice active listening: When people are talking, are you listening to respond or listening to fully grasp what they are sharing? There's a difference! To actively listen, you must focus in deeply on what is being shared. By actively listening you can learn more about others and ask relevant questions to keep the conversation going.

Watch how people move: A person's actions will tell you a lot more about them than their words. As you engage with people, especially in the workplace, take note of their actions. Do they keep their word? How do they treat others? Do they gossip a lot? By watching how people operate, you can make a well-rounded determination of their character.

Part 3

Exit Your Job
Like a Boss

CHAPTER 16

Plan the Next Step of Your Journey

When I transferred from Baltimore City Community College to Morgan State University in 2011, a gentleman who facilitated the new student orientation gave the incoming students some wise words that I probably will never forget. He asked us to think deeply about the work we wanted to do and the places we wanted to work. He told us to make a list of employer names, positions, salaries, experience needed, and other qualifications. This outline was supposed to help us establish our journey into the professional world. Ultimately, he wanted us to think long-term about where our education would take us.

At the time, it was hard for me to put a finger on exactly where I wanted to work and the specific type of work I wanted to engage in. However, I did know two things: I wanted to write, and I wanted to benefit Black people in some explicit way. This helped me get opportunities writing for the *Afro-American* newspaper, *Black Enterprise* magazine, and various other print and digital publications.

My message is to be conscious of where you want to go in the future, even if you are not fully sure of every fine detail. It is better to have an idea of where you want to go than to have no clue at all. When you are working at a job as a teenager, chances are that job will not be your end goal in life. You may start by working as a cashier or server, but your passions may lie elsewhere in the future. It is important for you to think long-term.

If you want to be a professional athlete, you need to think about more than just the money. You need to think about and be fully dedicated to obtaining your education, conditioning your body, studying contracts, talking to other professionals for advice, and learning all you can about your dream profession. It takes time, patience, and a tremendous amount of sacrifice. You need to also know that only a small percentage of college athletes go pro. With that in mind, you need to think of a backup plan to transfer your time and energy into if sports are no longer an option.

Sometimes it can be hard to think about what's next. I know for me it was. When I got my first job, I was unsure of what my next professional move would be. I was satisfied with just making a little bit of money to support my wants. I was not thinking about saving, creating a bank account, investing, starting a family, establishing a business, or anything long-term. I lived in the now—an unsafe space to solely exist in. If you fail to prepare, it will make the journey much more difficult.

Below Are Some Ideas to Consider as You Begin to Plan the Next Step on Your Employment Journey:

Take inventory of what your passions are and what careers align with those passions: If you like to draw, think about the artistic careers connected to that skill. If you love rebuilding computers, maybe an IT route is the way to go. The important takeaway here is to write your ideas down. Put them up in your room. Reference them often, and discover what actions you need to take in order to make those ideas into your reality.

Ask your parents, guardians, and mentors about how to plan for the future: There are adults all around you who have successfully transitioned into professional life. Have you asked them how they got started? Do you know their journeys? Pick one person per week to talk to about how they mapped out their plan and what it took to get them to where they are now.

Talk with your managers, supervisors, and others in positions of power about how they got into their positions: After you finish talking to professionals in your personal sphere, start to expand out into people in your professional networks. They may have really helpful advice to share with you.

Update your résumé: Are you feeling like you're in a place where you are ready to move on from your current employer? If so, it's time to update that résumé! Go visit your local library or workforce development center to get your résumé revised. Be ready to share new skills, certifications, and knowledge you have gained from your current workplace.

Think about being the owner of something rather than simply working to fulfill someone else's dream: Listen, it's cool to be an employee and work for somebody else, especially a Black-owned business. There is a tremendous amount of pride in earning a steady paycheck from an employer. Additionally, as you think long-term, you want to consider what it would take to start your own business. Are you learning skills that you could apply to starting your own enterprise? This idea should not be farfetched. If you choose this path, being an entrepreneur is a viable option.

CHAPTER 17

Exchange Contact Information with Important People

Oftentimes, employees underestimate the power and necessity of professional relationships. I can't tell you how many times I have met impactful people I barely conversed with. A part of it was me being shy, but another part of this was from me not seeing people as assets. Now, I am not saying you have to exchange numbers with everyone you meet. However, there are some people you should absolutely stay in contact with. As a teen, you should work to learn this lesson early and practice it often. Before leaving any job, internship, or even an extracurricular activity, you should get the contact information of people you deem as worthy of further communication. You don't need the number of everyone you've ever worked with stored in your iPhone, but you should take some time to think through who has connections and who may have access to other opportunities that can benefit you in the future. Inversely, think about who you can benefit and possibly support in the future. The relationship should be reciprocal.

If you can answer "yes" to any of the questions below, you should make sure to get someone's phone number, email address, and/or social media credentials.

Questions to consider:

- Does the person have a connection to other employers, internships, or other opportunities that can propel me up the professional ladder?
- Does the person have ideas that could potentially become a business I would want to be involved in?
- Did the person and I have good conversations and challenge each other to be greater?
- Could this person be a reference for me in the future?

When I graduated from Morgan State University in 2013, my first full-time job was as an AmeriCorps Community Service-Learning fellow. I worked fifty to sixty hours per week for below minimum wage for an entire year. The work was tiring, and I was broke. My car's struts and shocks were nonexistent, and every time my vehicle hit a bump in the road—which is every ten seconds in Baltimore—my car bounced like I was in a Snoop Dogg video. My car's heating system also stopped working in the middle of winter, so I had to warn people that they might freeze to death when they entered my car. Needless to say, it was a rough time in my life.

Even though I was living in poverty and taking full advantage of food stamps, I was able to smile and persevere thanks to the support of some of the dopest co-workers in the world. My team, the Jobs Team, was full of talented individuals I knew

I had to keep in contact with. They were not just hardworking employees. They had visions for transforming the landscape of Maryland and empowering others in the process. From politicians and educators to business owners and college access specialists, the people on this team became more than just my co-workers. They became a major part of my social capital. To this day, we still get together on a quarterly basis to laugh, eat, and provide each other with life updates. As a professional, you have to figure out who you value and who you should remain connected with.

CHAPTER 18

Don't Just Quit Your Job

When I was seventeen, my dad worked to get me a job at Stop Shop Save. He had a friend who was a regional manager, and I was lucky to not have to interview for the job. I talked to the regional manager for a few minutes and was hired on the spot. It was one of those job opportunities that just fell in my lap.

My first day on the job was long and tiring. There were a ton of things to learn, and my supervisor was a grumpy lady who hardly ever smiled. If I slouched, she would urge me to "stand up straight," and if I did something incorrect on the register, I could feel her eyes searing into the side of my head like laser beams. My second day on the job was the worst. I was bagging up some products purchased by a customer and ignorantly put cat food in the same bag as produce. The customer questioned my judgment and made me feel stupid. Even more humiliating, my supervisor was standing right there, shaking her head in disgust at my work performance. After I clocked out that day, I never went back. After two days of struggling on the job, I decided it was time to retire from the supermarket business. Now that I think about it, I didn't even get a paycheck from that job.

I had another part-time job at a bookstore, so I wasn't tripping about the loss of money from this job. Additionally, because this job was given to me without any work on my part, I did not value it much. All I knew was that I was out!

Weeks later, I ended up running into the regional manager. She apparently found out about my bookstore job from my dad and decided to come pay me a visit. I was trying to avoid her by staying upstairs when my manager told me she was downstairs to see me. I was hoping she would just leave and go on about her day. Well, that didn't happen. She came upstairs and asked me why I abruptly stopped working at the job she connected me with. I told her about my struggles and let her know I appreciated the opportunity, but I wasn't feeling the job anymore. She listened and shook her head. She then thanked me for my time and left. I never saw or spoke to her again after that.

Years later and after deep reflection, I realized that I had dropped the ball in many ways. For one, my dad was probably embarrassed that I quit without a two-week notice or any sense of responsibility. The regional manager was a friend of his. I may have caused a strain in their relationship. Secondly, I eliminated the possibility of adding this job to my résumé and having my supervisor from Stop Shop Save as a professional reference.

In the job world, much of your upward mobility is based on your connections with people. Sure, education and experience can get you a long way, but networking and being intentional about maintaining a professional network has put many people in places they would not have otherwise been. This is the lesson I learned from all of this, and this is what I want you to internalize. It is extremely important for you to end a job on a positive note. Even if you despise your supervisor or co-workers and hate the very thought of your employer, you should work to resign from your position without conflict and within a reasonable amount of time.

Below Are Some Tips on How to Leave Your Job on a Positive Note:

Give at least a two-week notice before resigning: This allows you to have a credible reference and résumé addition, in most cases. This also gives your employer time to prepare for your transition.

Talk with your supervisor about wrapping up projects/ assignments: You should never leave with a ton of incomplete work. It is imperative that you talk to your manager about how you can gracefully wrap up your responsibilities and pass along your work to the person who will take your place. In some cases, you may not be able to close out every project or assignment. Communicate with your supervisor if this is the case.

Give other employees word of your pending departure: There is nothing worse than being somewhere one day and then being gone the next. Your co-workers deserve to know that you are leaving, especially if their work will be impacted by your absence. You certainly don't have to elaborate as far as the "why" of you leaving, but you should at least give people a heads-up. This can happen at an all-staff meeting or through an organization-wide email. This should only be done after you have talked to your direct supervisor.

Conclusion

A job is not just a job. A job presents you with an opportunity to earn an income, feed your family, pay your bills, learn new skills, network, and improve your overall life trajectory. Whether you decide to work for "the man" or a Black-owned business, you should be ready to engage in every part of the job process and be willing to continue to learn along the journey. You should be talking about the topics in this book regularly—with your friends, family members, classmates, co-workers, and ultimately yourself. I want you to become obsessed with becoming the best version of yourself, and that includes improving your ability to navigate employment.

You can't leave success up to chance and wing it in hopes of your dream job falling in your lap. Things don't generally work that way outside of Disney movies. Before starting a job, update or create your résumé, create and check your email address, update your social media pages, understand the dress standards of that industry, and embrace the greatness you possess as a Black teen. It's also essential to be knowledgeable of the various forms of discrimination that may attempt to hinder your progress.

Once you secure a job, that is not the end of your journey. It's not about simply getting the job; it's about keeping it and excelling. While on the job, you should look for opportunities to acquire new skills, travel, network, and learn about the practices and policies of your workplace. Are you and others being treated with respect and dignity? While working, keep your eyes and ears open to your environment.

On Jay-Z's "Encore," he raps, "Grand opening, grand closing." That's the type of mentality that will build your name and overall credibility. You should start strong and finish strong. What do you want the company to say about you when you're gone? Though you can't completely control this narrative, your answer should determine your actions while working there.

I'll be real with you. The world, including the American job market, is unbalanced, and its current construction is not set up for the majority of non-white people to thrive. COVID-19 magnified the workplace inequities that plague employees of color, especially low-wage workers. I know a number of people who were terminated from their jobs or, alternatively, had to risk their lives to travel to workplaces where there were multiple confirmed COVID-19 cases. When it comes to employment, millions of people do not have the option to telework or even take off when they are ill. This is not the reality for all, though. In fact, according to the Institute for Policy Studies, since mid-March, while 40 million Americans filed for unemployment, US billionaires had a wealth increase of $584 billion.

Low-wage workers of color are the least valued employees in this country. It hurts, and I hate even having to write these words. It has been this way for some time. Some fifty years ago, Dr. Martin Luther King Jr. spent the last days of his life working on behalf of Black workers facing wage discrimination.

Anti-blackness and other forms of discrimination in the workplace are real. Through policy and practice, they are as American as apple pie. However, I want you to know that today, in this moment in history, it is your duty to be observant and challenge unjust practices. You should also know that you are not in this alone and there are people, resources, and organizations available to assist you. Some of them are noted throughout this book.

There will never be a time in life where the world slows down in order for you to get serious about navigating employment. There is no better time than the present. Whether you want to work at Foot Locker, like I did, or you're seeking some other job or career path, it's time to take inventory of what you have and what you don't have when it comes to employment. Once you know where you stand, you can then create and execute a plan to become the best young Black professional you can be.

Resource Guide

Websites

- Youth@Work/US Equal Employment Opportunity Commission: eeoc.gov/youth. Understanding youth rights and responsibilities within the workforce
- YouthRules!: youthrules.gov. Information to promote positive, safe work experiences for teens
- Gmail: gmail.com. Free, web-based email service provided by Google
- Public Libraries: publiclibraries.com: A directory of public libraries within the US
- Miss Write on Time: misswriteontime.com. Premium career development services
- Mint: mint.com. Free personal finance service
- LinkedIn: linkedin.com. A social network for professionals
- Associated Black Charities: abc-md.org. A nonprofit advocating for racial equity for African Americans in Maryland
- Job Opportunities Task Force: jotf.org. A leading voice in fighting for low-wage workers in Maryland

Books

- Neely Fuller: *The United-Independent Compensatory Code/System/Concept Textbook: A Compensatory Counter-Racist Code*
- Charmanique Anderson: *Who Likes Résumé Writing Anyway?*
- Sam Greenlee: *The Spook Who Sat By the Door*
- Reginald F. Lewis: *Why Should White Guys Have All the Fun?: How Reginald Lewis Created a Billion-Dollar Business Empire*
- Jason Reynolds and Ibram X. Kendi: *Stamped: Racism, Antiracism, and You*
- Dr. Amos Wilson: *Blueprint for Black Power: A Moral, Political, and Economic Imperative for the Twenty-First Century*
- Angela Davis: *Freedom is a Constant Struggle: Ferguson, Palestine, and the Foundations of a Movement*
- Minda Harts: *The Memo: What Women of Color Need to Know to Secure a Seat at the Table*
- Donald Clifton, Edward Anderson, and Laurie Schreiner: *StrengthsQuest: Discover and Develop Your Strengths in Academics, Career, and Beyond*
- Dennis Kimbro and Napoleon Hill: *Think and Grow Rich: A Black Choice*
- Mindy Bingham and Sandy Stryker: *Career Choices: A Guide for Teens and Young Adults*

Music & Poems

- "I'm Black"–Styles P
- "Alright"–Kendrick Lamar
- "HiiiPoWeR"–Kendrick Lamar
- "Beautiful Struggle"–Talib Kweli
- "We Wear the Mask"–Paul Laurence Dunbar
- "I Talk Black"–Lady Brion
- "The Bigger Picture"–Lil Baby
- "What's Free"–Meek Mill
- "Love Yourz"–J. Cole
- "Bigger Than Me"–Big Sean
- "Still I Rise"–Maya Angelou
- "Mastermind"–Nas
- "Spaceship"–Kanye West

Acknowledgments

First of all, I want to acknowledge the creator of all things who goes by many names. I am extremely blessed to know that I was created by a higher being that helps guide my mind and heart.

To my family members and friends, thank you for believing in me. I told some of y'all about my ideas for this book, and y'all gave me the kind words and motivation I needed to make it happen. This is a win for our tribe!

To all my teachers and mentors, thank you all for pouring into me. I have been blessed by so many wise educators, upright professionals, and astute elders. Please accept these roses while you are still here. You deserve them.

To my dad, thank you for showing me manhood. I can't even count all the lessons I've learned from listening to you and being in your presence. I love you, Baba.

To Aisha, I remember sitting on the couch in our apartment talking through this idea with you. I read the unfinished preface of the book to you, and I bounced a bunch of ideas off you in the early stages. Those conversations were pivotal to the development of this book. I love you and can't wait to marry you.

To Granny, Delores Noble, thank you for being the most caring person I know. You demonstrate empathy and joy every day.

To Baltimore, you continue to groom and challenge me. I will continue the fight of improving you and making you what you should be.

To my editor, Lindsey Alexander, thank you for helping me execute this project. I believe that every writer needs an editor in order to make magic happen. Your power of words is astounding!

To my cover designer, Mikea Hugley, you are a graphic designing beast! We had so many conversations to get this right, and it was all worth it. It's crazy that I found you by looking up who designed Kondwani Fidel's books. It was ordained for us to connect!

To my Kickstarter backers, y'all are the best support system in the world! Thank you for pledging, spreading the word, and fully funding this book project! Y'all helped me raise $4,814 to create this book. I'm still in awe. #GodsPlan

To Black youth everywhere, keep being dope, and stiff-arm those haters out of your life. It's your time to win. Own it!

And last but not least, to everyone who purchased, shared, and read this book, I pray it was worth your time and money. I hope you enjoyed learning about parts of my employment journey. These stories were fun to retell and process as an adult. Congratulations, you are now a part of my family.

References

Campbell, Alexia Fernández. "California Is about to Ban Discrimination against Black Workers with Natural Hairstyles." Vox. Vox, July 3, 2019. www.vox.com/ identities/2019/7/3/20680946/california-crown-act -natural-hair-discrimination.

Chuck, Elizabeth. "Former Hooters Waitress Awarded $250,000 in Racial Discrimination Case." NBCNews.com. NBCUniversal News Group, June 11, 2015. www.nbcnews .com/news/us-news/former-hooters-waitress-awarded -250-000-racial-discrimination-case-n337396.

Clemente, Deirdre. "Why American Workers Now Dress So Casually." The Atlantic. Atlantic Media Company, May 22, 2017. www.theatlantic.com/business/archive/2017/05/ history-of-business-casual/526014/.

Collins, Chuck. "US Billionaire Wealth Surges to $584 Billion, or 20 Percent, Since the Beginning of the Pandemic." Institute for Policy Studies, June 19, 2020. https://ips-dc. org/us-billionaire-wealth-584-billion-20-percent -pandemic/.

"Employment and Unemployment Among Youth Summary." US Bureau of Labor Statistics. US Bureau of Labor Statistics, August 16, 2019. https://www.bls.gov/news. release/youth.nr0.htm.

"Employment Situation News Release." US Bureau of Labor Statistics. US Bureau of Labor Statistics, July 2, 2020. www.bls.gov/news.release/archives/empsit_07022020.htm.

Gerdeman, Dina. "Minorities Who 'Whiten' Job Resumes Get More Interviews." HBS Working Knowledge, May 17, 2017. https://hbswk.hbs.edu/item/minorities-who-whiten -job-resumes-get-more-interviews.

Jameel, Maryam, and Joe Yerardi. "Workplace Discrimination Is Illegal. But Our Data Shows It's Still a Huge Problem." Vox. Vox, February 28, 2019. www.vox.com/policy-and -politics/2019/2/28/18241973/workplace-discrimination -cpi-investigation-eeoc.

"JAY-Z – Encore." Genius, November 14, 2003. https://genius. com/Jay-z-encore-lyrics.

"Overview." US Equal Employment Opportunity Commission. Accessed August 9, 2020. https://www.eeoc.gov/overview.

"Relaxation Techniques: Breath Control Helps Quell Errant Stress Response." Harvard Health Publishing. Harvard University, January 2015. https://www.health.harvard.edu/ mind-and-mood/relaxation-techniques-breath-control -helps-quell-errant-stress-response.

Salm, Lauren. "70% Of Employers Are Snooping Candidates' Social Media Profiles." CareerBuilder, June 15, 2017. www.careerbuilder.com/advice/social-media-survey-2017.

"Writing a Good Resume: Student Critique and Practice Exercise." Writing a Good Resume: Student Exercise | Education World, May 19, 2017. www.educationworld. com/a_lesson/writing-good-resume-career-readiness. shtml.

About the Author

Albert Phillips Jr. works as a Work-Based Learning Specialist with Baltimore City Public Schools. He specializes in urban education and youth development. Albert earned a Master of Science degree in Education from Johns Hopkins University and a Bachelor of Science degree in Journalism from Morgan State University. His work has appeared in *Black Enterprise*, *NewsOne*, *The Afro-American*, and various other digital and print publications. Albert resides in Baltimore.